Get in the Game! With Robin Roberts

CAREERS

for Women Who Love

SPORTS

The Millbrook Press   Brookfield, Connecticut

The author and publisher wish to thank
Bill Gutman for his research and writing
contributions to this series.

Published by The Millbrook Press, Inc.
2 Old New Milford Road
Brookfield, Connecticut 06804
www.millbrookpress.com

Library of Congress Cataloging-in-Publication
Data
Roberts, Robin, 1960–
Careers for women who love sports.
p. cm. – (Get in the game! With Robin Roberts)
Includes bibliographical references and index.
Summary: Seven women discuss their work in
various sports-related careers, including referee,
athletic trainer, agent, writer, and nutritionist,
and describe the skills and education needed.
ISBN 0-7613-1408-3 (lib. bdg.) – ISBN 0-7613-
1282-X (pbk.)
1. Sports for women—vocational guidance—
United States—Juvenile literature (1. Sports for
women—Vocational guidance. 2. Sports—
Vocational guidance. 3. Vocational guidance. 4.
Women—Employment.) I. Title.
GV709 R63 2000 796'.023'73—dc21 99-046221

CONTENTS

Introduction

Sports has always been a big part of my life. From playing sandlot football with the other kids in my neighborhood in Biloxi, Mississippi, to playing tennis in high school and basketball in college, to working in sports broadcasting at ESPN, I can't imagine my life without sports. It used to be that girls who played sports were labeled "tomboys." These days, however, women and sports go hand-in-hand in so many ways.

Sports can increase a girl's confidence and help her to feel good about herself, and can help her succeed in nearly every aspect of life including school, a career, and relationships with friends and family.

With **Get in the Game!** my goal is to share my love and knowledge of the world of sports, and to show just how important sports can be. What you can learn on the field, court, rink, and arena are ways to solve problems, communicate with others, and become a leader. No matter what your skill level, if you learn all that sports can teach you, how can you *not* succeed at life in general? And the best part is that, like I have, you'll have fun at the same time!

—Robin Roberts

How Can I Make a Career Out of SPORTS?

Like so many people, you love sports. Maybe basketball is your game. Maybe tennis or volleyball. Or maybe you love all sports, and plan to make a career out of your love for sports. The good news is that even if you aren't one of the lucky few who wind up being a star in the WNBA or a world-class figure skater or a pro golfer competing in big-money tournaments, there are many other rewarding ways to make a career out of sports.

Throughout the 1980s and 1990s, more girls and women were participating in sports than ever before. And not only were there more opportunities for women to play sports, there were also opportunities to prepare for many sports-related careers, as well.

Some of these careers may be familiar to you; others may not. Women have been successful in all of them. Some sports-related careers, such as coaching and officiating, involve working directly with players or being on the court or field with them during games. Others, such as journalism, broadcasting, and athletic training, often require the participant to be at the games. Still others, such as nutrition counseling, and marketing and public relations usually have a work venue away from the action much of the time. But all of these careers are necessary to help keep sports running. In this book, women in seven sports-related careers, including me, will describe their work. Through our words, you'll learn about what it takes to be successful in a sports career. Each of us loves the work we do. And like you, each of us is passionate about sports.

Many of these sports-related fields used to be the exclusive domain of men. Some of the women you'll read about are pioneers who have worked very hard to prove that they could do the job as well as or better than a man could. In doing so, they have paved the way for the women who followed.

Being successful at any career, including a career in sports, isn't easy, even if it's your passion. But if you think you might want to be a coach, official, athletic trainer, nutritionist, public relations or marketing specialist, journalist, or broadcaster, read on to find out how to get there and how to succeed.

Val Ackerman
worked in the National Basketball Association (NBA) for eight years before she became president of the WNBA. A former college basketball player, she took her love for the game and turned it into a lifelong career.

Coach Nell Fortner gets a lift from her Team USA players after their victory over Russia in the 1998 World Championship Finals. One quality good coaches have, Fortner says, is compassion—athletes often have many things going on in their lives, and a coach has to have an understanding of each player on the team.

1 Coach

Nell Fortner is the first full-time coach of the United States Women's National Basketball Team. This is the team that competes in the World Championships, the Pan American Games, and other international competitions, as well as in the Olympic Games. A former player at the University of Texas, Fortner came up through the coaching ranks, starting at the high school level. She then was an assistant coach at Steven F. Austin University, Louisiana Tech University and with the 1995–1996 National Team that won the Gold Medal at the 1996 Summer Olympic Games in Atlanta. Next she became the head coach at Purdue University before returning to USA Basketball and the National Team.

If you want to coach, you should play. This doesn't mean that you have to be a collegiate star, or even a star in high school. But you should play the sport you feel you want to coach at some level. Playing gives you an edge because you'll know how the players feel while they're on the court. You'll have a better idea of what they're going through.

For those who don't play but still want to coach, try to be as close to the game as you can by being a team manager, a scorer, or a student assistant. If you can get close to the game in any way, you'll pick up experience by listening to what the coaches say and watching them work.

With basketball—as well as most other sports—there are more coaching opportunities at the high school and college levels. Ohio State University, for example, has 35 varsity sports for both men and women.

Education is of prime importance when competing for a job. In fact, many coaching positions at the college level require a master's degree. There is no degree given in coaching, so you can study other subjects in college. For instance, you can have a degree in history and be a coach. But physical education is a good major to consider if you know you want to coach.

What qualities do you need to be a good coach? I think you have to start with a real love for your sport and never feel that it is work. In other words, you need to have a passion for the game. This will help you to be enthusiastic. Your players will feed off your enthusiasm and want to work hard for you.

As a coach, you've got to get every one of your players to be the best she can be every time out. Part of that is being a good motivator; finding ways to make your players push themselves to play their best and win.

Coaches must also be teachers. Listen and learn as you grow. Pick up knowledge and experience everywhere you can. Everything you learn will enable you to better relate the game to your players. Try to attend special summer sports camps and learn directly from coaches who teach at them. There are summer camps for future players and coaches in many sports all over the country.

Coaching at the high school level

or below often means being a full-time teacher, as well. There are many opportunities for coaching students of all ages in many different settings, but usually these coaching jobs are part-time. Coaching at younger levels can be a great way to indulge your love for sports while pursuing another career. Here, a middle-school softball coach instructs some of her players.

Utah Starzz coach Denise Taylor consults with player Chantel Tremitiere in a WNBA game against the Los Angeles Sparks.

instance, might spend several hours watching films or tapes and preparing for practice. She may then spend a few hours writing recruiting letters and talking to high school coaches about prospective players. There has to be time set aside for administrative duties—talking to players, making up game plans, or spending time with the school's athletic director.

Before practice, a coach will spend an hour or so with her assistants. After conducting a three-hour practice session, there may be another couple of hours' work watching films of opponents, your own team's practices, opponents' games, or your own games. During the season there is a great deal of travel, both to games and to look at possible recruits.

Coaching is hard work. A college coach will often work 10 to 12 hours a day. A basketball coach, for

High school coaches don't have to worry about recruiting, but they must also teach classes. They spend a good deal of the school day responsible for students other than their athletes. Then it's on to coaching, with practices often held after school or even at night. High school coaches must also do the same kind of game preparation and handling of individual players that college coaches do.

As a coach, I would say the most satisfaction comes from winning. But I enjoy every part of my job. I enjoy dealing with the different personalities on my teams. It's a challenge to get each and every girl to work hard and to feel good about herself.

The hardest part of the job is losing, especially when your team doesn't perform up to its ability. You have to ask yourself why they didn't play well and, as the coach, you must take the blame. It's also not always easy dealing with players' problems. For instance, if a player isn't happy about the amount of game time she's getting, it can become a distraction to the whole team. You must know how to handle it.

My advice to future coaches is simple: Be the best you can be in school. Gather all the information you can. You might want to even keep a coaching notebook. Become a good communicator so you can teach and talk to your players. Become a motivator so your players will work for you. Care about your players and love the game with a passion. Then set a goal and work hard to achieve it. And when you reach one goal, immediately set another. I set a goal of becoming the Olympic basketball coach by the year 2008. I reached my goal early because I really believed it would happen.

2 Official

Dee Kantner was one of the first women ever to referee in the National Basketball Association (NBA). She began working NBA games in the 1997–1998 season, and is a pioneer of her profession. She was an official in National Collegiate Athletic Association (NCAA) Women's Division I basketball for 13 years. Before that, she worked Division II games for a year and spent several years honing her skills at the high school level. Today she works in the NBA full time and is also qualified to officiate at the international level during the NBA off-season.

Most women who want to become sports officials know they can't do it as a full-time profession. In pro basketball, for instance, there are only 57 jobs available in the NBA and fewer in the WNBA. If you want to become an official, my advice is to get a good education and work toward another profession, while you officiate as a hobby. You can ref college ball evenings and weekends, making extra money while working full time at another job.

In many countries, youngsters are encouraged to begin officiating at a very young age. That doesn't happen in the United States. I've gone to high school sports camps and asked how many of the campers want to be refs. Sometimes not a single hand has gone up. Then I'll ask them to give me 20 minutes. Hopefully I can convince them in that time that officiating is an exciting occupation.

It certainly is helpful to future officials to play the game they want to officiate, but it isn't a requirement. I've been playing basketball since I was seven, and played one year in college. The years of being on the court as a player gave me an extra feel for the game.

While some colleges have courses in officiating, you cannot earn a degree in it. But remember

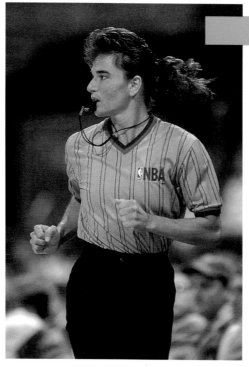

Dee Kantner, NBA referee, in action. She calls herself a "physical-fitness fanatic" and says she never stops working out. It has helped tremendously in her career.

that wherever there's a game, there has to be a ref—so there are plenty of opportunities to gain experience. Even when you are in high school you can begin officiating in town or church leagues. Later, you can begin working Little League and Pop Warner ball, or in age-group soccer leagues.

There are camps to train future officials in many different sports— basketball, softball, field hockey, and soccer, to name just a few. Supervisors of officials for the differ-

One of the great things about officiating is that there are so many opportunities—it can be done at any level, in any sport, from little-league baseball on up to professional basketball.

ent college conferences often go to the camps to find new officials. If you live on the East Coast, for instance, you can do some research and find out at which camp the supervisor of officials from the Big East will attend. If he likes the way you work, you may have a chance to become a Big East official.

If you're good at what you do, and attend a lot of camps, the word will get around. People will hear about you and you will begin getting better assignments. In that sense, you can take control of your own destiny by going to the best places to be seen as an official.

To be an official in any sport, you must keep yourself in top physical condition. Basketball, hockey, and soccer officials, for example, must do a lot of moving during games. If you're huffing and puffing, you won't be able to concentrate on your job. That means you've got to find a very good workout program and keep at it.

An official also has to have a strong sense of self-esteem because, in calling a game, not everyone is going to like you. You've also got to have a good sense of humor and not take yourself too seriously.

You've also got to have a thorough knowledge of the rules so you can properly defend any controversial calls you make and keep control of the game. A solid work ethic is also necessary for success. One game is not more important than any other from the standpoint of the official. You've got to remember that every game you call is very important to the participating athletes.

And finally, you must respect the players and coaches. If you are

WNBA referees "hold court" with some players and members of the media before game time. Officials can sometimes seem all powerful, but Dee Kantner stresses that while a referee needs to take her responsibilities seriously, she can't be on an ego or power trip. A good official always remembers that the game is not about her.

respectful to everyone, chances are they will be more respectful to you.

The hardest part of my job as an NBA official is the travel—being on the road almost constantly, going from city to city. At other levels, the travel isn't as grueling. You may be officiating near your home and just have to travel to surrounding towns. College officials must travel further, but they are not full-time officials and do not spend nearly as much time traveling. Other than the games, there are sometimes meetings with fellow officials or your supervisor, and game reports to fill out.

As an official, you are going to have to make a number of close calls that can go in either team's favor. You've got to be right on the play and have the confidence to make an immediate decision. If you don't get a clear view of a play, then you can look to a fellow official for help.

You must also be prepared to deal with pressure. If you're working a big game with the score tied, the clock ticking down, and 20,000 fans screaming in the stands, you've got to be ready to get the play right. That's what you're being paid to do. You can't worry about the fans—they're going to see it the way they want to.

There are always a lot of people—fans, players, coaches—playing mind games with you out there. Some call it "ref baiting." You can't be affected by what you hear. For me, that kind of pressure is an exciting part of the job.

Being a basketball official is a great occupation. It can also be a great hobby, but only if you enjoy it and love the sport you're working. Once you lose the fun of any job, it's time to get a new one.

3 Sports Journalist

Sally Jenkins is a senior contributing writer for Women's Sports & Fitness magazine, as well as a contributor to ESPN, Tennis, and other magazines. She began her writing career in California while studying at Stanford University, working part-time for the Palo Alto Times. After graduation, she began covering high school sports for the San Francisco Examiner, then worked for three other newspapers, including the Washington Post. From there, she spent seven years as a writer for Sports Illustrated. She is also the author of four books.

By the time I joined the *Washington Post* in 1984, there were quite a number of women journalists writing about sports. But it was only three or four years earlier that the field really began to open up for women.

The first women to enter the field of sports journalism were really pioneers. Even today, there's a lingering feeling among some women that they don't know as much about sports as men and, as a result, they don't have as much self-confidence as they should. But if you grow up in a sports atmosphere, play sports a great deal while you're growing up,

Sally Jenkins (fourth from left) is joined by other sports journalists, as well as soccer star Julie Foudy (right), at a Women's Sports Foundation gathering. One of the most rewarding aspects of Jenkins's job is writing stories about misunderstood figures. "A writer who does her job well," she says, "can make the reader sympathize with and understand a public figure much better."

and even play alongside and against boys, there's no reason to feel you don't know as much.

Writing about sports isn't easy. It's a lot more than just telling who won and who lost a game. Sports journalism today can involve a number of complex topics such as labor disputes, drug problems, sex crimes, social problems, financial issues, and others.

There are many things you can do to get your career as a sports

Lesley Visser, after establishing herself as a sports journalist in the newspaper world, jumped to television broadcasting. Here she gets up close and personal with San Francisco 49ers quarterback Steve Young.

can "hear" what you read, begin to feel the rhythm of the words, and the way sentences and paragraphs are put together. If you have the radio blasting or the TV on in the background, you won't get the total reading experience and you won't learn as much from the writing.

There are a number of other things you can do to get early writing experience. Most schools have their own newspapers. Join the staff. If your school doesn't have a paper, talk to your teachers about starting one. By working on a school paper, you'll not only get valuable writing experience, but will learn about deadlines, page setup, and other workings of a newspaper. Outside of

writer started early. The first is to write—every day if you can. Keep a diary or journal, write letters, take care when writing school assignments, and write to your friends via e-mail. There are many ways to practice.

Any aspiring writer should also enjoy reading a great deal. Try to read in a quiet setting. That way, you school, you and some of your friends might think about starting a neighborhood newsletter.

My father, journalist and novelist Dan Jenkins, used to copy stories from the newspaper when he was a kid. As he got older, he began rewriting the sports stories in his own style. There are many ways to practice your writing. Find what works best for you and keep at it.

Today, a college education is vital if you want to be a sports journalist. Journalism is certainly a good major for an aspiring writer, though majoring in English is also a good idea. Even if you know you want to write about sports, it will benefit you to learn about other things, like economics, history, and social studies. Knowledge is an indispensable tool for a writer, so your education will not only help you find a job,

but will help you immeasurably in your work.

You also need to learn how to gather material and facts accurately. Research can be tedious and often requires a great deal of unglamorous legwork, but it's an important part of being a writer.

Daily newspaper work has to be done quickly. You must learn to research and write your story fast. If, for example, you're doing a preview story on a big game to be held the next day, you might start by going out and watching the home team practice. Then you'll need to talk to the players and coaches about the mood of the team, and maybe have them evaluate their opponent.

Back at the office you might call the opposing team and try to speak with a player or coach to get their view on the game and on the local team. At this point you might have about two hours to write the story and get it in for the next day's edition. For a newspaper, you're always working on a tight deadline.

By contrast, if you're writing a feature story for a magazine such as *Sports Illustrated*, you may have anywhere from two to four weeks to complete the assignment. Suppose you are writing about Dallas Cowboys quarterback Troy Aikman. After you receive permission to conduct the interview and have set up a time to do so, you would fly to Dallas and meet Troy. You would then have an interview session, perhaps at his home. You might return the next day and spend more time with him, perhaps playing golf or participating in some other relaxed activity. Then you would do another interview.

But you're still not finished.

You've also got to talk to people around him, maybe a family member, his coach, and several teammates. You'll often find that others have valuable insights into the person you're writing about. They will help you get a more complete portrait of your subject. Then comes the writing process, which may involve three or four days of hard writing. After you submit the story, your editor may then ask for changes or revisions, which you must do quickly.

Writing a book is still another story. If you're working with an individual or a team to tell a life story or the story of a complete season, you almost have to live with your subject for months on end. Your research involves knowing the subject so well that you almost feel a part of it. And the writing process can literally take months and months of hard work.

Lisa Olsen, a writer for the New York Daily News, on assignment at a New York Knicks NBA playoff game in 1999.

A sports journalist must be energetic, hardworking, tireless with a high energy level, and dogged in her pursuit of a story. Writing is often a solitary job and can be a lonely one, but there are many rewards. You'll learn the pleasure of self-expression. You also become something of a voice of the people, communicating to many.

I've always loved doing feature stories on people who are not very well understood. A writer who does a good job can make a reader sympathize and understand public figures much better. That's one of the major rewards of being a writer. I still tell young people that female sports writers may sometimes be picked on by guys. But even a negative experience can build character and understanding. If you feel something isn't fair, don't complain. Do something about it.

4 Athletic Trainer

Karen Toburen is the department head and professor of sports medicine and athletic training at Southwest Missouri State University in Springfield, Missouri. Prior to that she spent 23 years at the University of Wisconsin at LaCrosse as an athletic trainer and curriculum director of the athletic training education program. She was also a member of the 1988 United States Olympic team medical staff and the athletic trainer for the 1988 U.S. Olympic women's basketball team. Toburen has a Doctorate of Education in the Behavioral Aspects of Sport.

People often ask me the difference between an athletic trainer and a physical therapist. I tell them that an athletic trainer deals more with physically active people and is on the sidelines during sporting events.

There was a time when almost all athletic trainers were men. But women's sports opened up at the collegiate level in the 1970s and the profession really exploded. The huge demand for trainers for women's sports teams brought more and more women into the field.

Athletic training programs are all-encompassing and combine academics with clinical experience that will prepare you for an exam that will

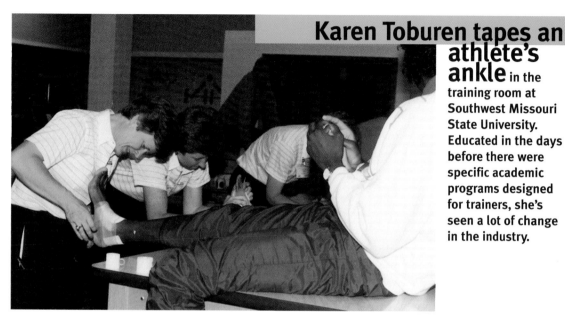

Karen Toburen tapes an athlete's ankle in the training room at Southwest Missouri State University. Educated in the days before there were specific academic programs designed for trainers, she's seen a lot of change in the industry.

certify you to work as an athletic trainer. The profession continues to grow. In the past, you could take just seven classes, put in 1,500 clinical hours, get a degree, take the exam, and be certified. But things are changing. By the year 2004, you will have to attend an accredited school if you want to become a certified athletic trainer.

Any athletic training career should begin with a love of sports.

Most trainers began by playing sports and enjoying the camaraderie they find with their teammates. Being an athlete helps also because it gives you a better understanding of sports and of the kinds of injuries that can occur.

Along with a love of sports, there should be an interest in science, especially in the human body, as well as a desire to provide health care to active sports participants.

Many larger high schools have trainers. If the trainers don't work full time, they often come in on a rotating basis and cover more than one school. You can ask to be a student trainer, or an observer when the athletic trainer is working. Once you begin college, you can shadow or observe classes as well as watch the trainers in action, maybe even work with them.

There are athletic training positions in professional sports, international sports such as the Olympics, at the college level, and in high schools. If you want to work at the high school level, it's advisable to take a double major—athletic training and an academic subject. That way, you can teach during the day and then serve as a trainer in the afternoon and sometimes evenings. (Only larger high schools, with teams at three or four different levels, have full time trainers. Unfortunately, it sometimes takes a serious sports-related injury or even a death to cause a school to wake up to the need for a full time athletic trainer.)

An athletic trainer has a great deal of responsibility. These responsibilities can be broken down into four basic categories. The first is to prevent injuries, the second is to manage injuries that do occur, the third is to rehabilitate injured athletes, and the fourth is to educate and counsel. These activities are all part of a trainer's daily and weekly routines.

The prevention phase of the job is divided into three parts—pre-season, the season itself, and post-season. Before the season begins, the trainer works with the coaches in mapping out a program to get the athletes ready. This usually involves flexibility training (stretching), strength training (weight work), and cardio-vascular conditioning (running).

During the season, the conditioning program must be modified to keep the athletes in top condition while they are performing. In the post-season, the concentration is on maintaining strength and flexibility while completely rehabilitating any injuries.

On the sidelines during the season, the trainer helps the athletes give an optimum performance and must be responsible for the management of injuries that occur during competition. When an athlete is hurt, the athletic trainer must make an immediate evaluation as to whether to allow that athlete back into the game or hold her out. The

Athletes depend on trainers to help keep their conditioning on track. A pregame stretch is just one of the important things a trainer can assist with.

rule of thumb is to avoid placing an athlete in a situation where she might sustain a serious injury. Statistics show that 7 or 8 percent of sports injuries can be life-threatening, so the trainer must always be ready with knowledge and know-how.

She must also be very familiar with all the latest equipment, such as knee and ankle braces, to decide whether the athlete can perform safely using the equipment to protect an injury. That means continuing to study and learn.

In the area of rehabilitation, the trainer has the responsibility of helping the athlete return to action following an injury or surgery. In this situation, the trainer will work one-on-one with an athlete. Again, the trainer must be familiar with surgical procedures—what was done,

what tissues were affected—and how the athlete can be brought back safely.

My advice to a young person thinking about becoming an athletic trainer is simple: Do well in school, study the basic sciences, as well as anatomy and physiology, and develop excellent writing and communication skills. You'll be working in a people industry. You'll be in a competitive college admissions program. Not everyone who applies to an athletic training program is accepted, so the more knowledge and experience you have, the better.

This is an exciting profession. You'll be working with people who love sports, and with athletes who don't want to be injured. But if they are, they are highly motivated to get back and will look to you to help them return safely.

5 Marketing Specialist

Sue Rodin has her own sports marketing and management company, Stars and Strategies, which specializes in women's sports and works with companies interested in sports consultation. The company represents a number of athletes in the areas of endorsements and appearances. Prior to running her own company, Rodin worked as an in-house consultant for Avon products, working on the company's Olympic program. She gained valuable experience working for a small sports marketing company, National Media Group (NMG), where her responsibilities included event management, promotion, and college marketing.

Marketing can include advertising, public relations, and direct mail, to promote brand, product, and company images. It's about positioning a product or service within the community or creating an identity for a product, person, or service.

There are many different kinds of jobs in the area of sports marketing. Some are public relations director at the college level or for a professional sports franchise, promotions manager for a corporation dealing with sportsware or sports products, and

Sue Rodin (second from left) also serves as president of an organization called Women in Sports and Events (WISE). Here she presents awards to (from left to right) track star Jackie Joyner-Kersee; Nancy Brinker, president of the Susan B. Koman Breast Cancer Foundation; and Pat Summit, head coach of the champion Tennessee Lady Vols college basketball team.

promotional director for an arena or venue that puts on sports events and promotions. Not only do companies that manufacture sports products need marketing people, but companies that want to be affiliated with athletes, sports products, and sports personalities also need sports marketing specialists.

I feel that almost all business skills are transferable to the sports area. So, no matter what part of marketing, promotion, public relations, or advertising that you study, you can make a career of it in sports.

The only requirement is that you have a genuine love for sports. If you play sports, all the better. But even if you don't, there are still ways you can be around sports from an early age. You can become a team manager, a statistician, or sports reporter for your school newspaper. If there are sporting events at a venue in your town or city, volunteer to be a part of it. "How can I help?" is a great phrase. There's always something to do, especially at site events where so much organization is needed.

The same things apply when you reach college. If you don't play sports, then manage a team or write about sports. Find out if any intern-ships are available. Students can often work in the college sports information office or report scores and game summaries to the local newspapers, or even the news wire services. Sometimes local compa-nies offer internships in their mar-keting departments. They don't have to be sports companies. Remember, any marketing skills you learn can be transferred to sports later.

There are a number of skills and qualities that are essential for a per-son to be successful in the sports marketing field. For starters, read and learn as much about sports as you can. If you want to concentrate on a particular sport, focus on that one. Get to know the athletes, the writers, the editors—as many involved people as possible. Try to develop strong writing and commu-nication skills.

You've also got to be creative and know how to get people interested in your ideas. You can't be afraid to make aggressive and confident pre-sentations. In public relations, espe-cially, you must be assertive without turning people off. It's a balance you have to find on your own. People in this business are very busy. You can seek advice from a mentor, but others won't babysit you. It's up to you to do your homework and show initiative.

As a public relations specialist, you will spend much of your time writing and speaking. The job involves dispensing information, which may take the form of news releases and media guides. Public relations people also have to speak to various groups. It may be at a press conference to make an announcement on behalf of your organization, then fielding questions from the audience. Or it may be giv-

Public relations work includes the preparation of media guides, which requires gathering information on players' lives and careers as well as the history of the team or franchise. Julie Fie (right) is the vice president of basketball communications for the NBA Phoenix Suns. She is pictured with a writer from *USA Today* and Suns star Jason Kidd (center).

ing a talk at a club or organization regarding the team or company you represent—to promote an event, or to talk about the team's value to the community.

Marketing can involve a fair amount of travel and some long workdays. If you represent a company, you've got to go to trade shows, where you make contacts, try to find new outlets for your product, and keep tabs on what the competition is doing. You might also go to conventions, such as the Women's

Sports Foundation's annual summit meeting. That will keep you up-to-date with the world of women's sports. My company also does a great deal of corporate work. For example, we worked with a new company that was putting together a mail-order catalog of apparel and equipment for female athletes. Our job was to provide a public relations and marketing strategy to promote the catalog and make sure it was seen by the greatest number of potential customers. One strategy we came up with was to do a cross-promotion with a new women's sports magazine. The magazine would promote the catalog, and the catalog would have a card inside inviting people to subscribe to the magazine.

A marketing person must learn all about the client's business and then look for opportunities to help it grow. In addition, you must always be out looking for new business and clients while making sure your current clients are happy.

The unglamorous part is all the paperwork. For example, after a meeting, at which you must be a very good listener and take notes, you need to write up the notes, then write memos to your staff so everyone knows who's doing what. You've then got to follow up with everyone so that you have complete knowledge of the entire procedure and everyone's role in it. But to help a company achieve success is very rewarding. And that's what sports marketing is all about.

Marketing specialists

attend annual trade shows like the Super Show, a sports-related convention. This marketing specialist (right) demonstrates some of the new sports products from the company she represents while potential customers look on.

6 Nutritionist

Heidi Skolnik is the president of Nutrition Conditioning, Inc., a nutrition and fitness consulting firm. She has master's degrees in exercise physiology and human nutrition and is a certified dietician/nutritionist. Among her clients are the New York Giants football team, the New York Mets baseball club, and the School of American Ballet. In addition, she is a contributing nutrition advisor for Women's Sports and Fitness magazine, as well as a consultant to the Hospital for Special Surgery/Women's Sports Medicine Center in New York City.

Sports nutrition is a fairly new field. In fact, when I went to school there were no classes in sports nutrition. But now students can major in nutrition and physiology (the workings of the human body). The two go hand-in-hand.

There are many skills a sports nutritionist must have if she is to be successful once she completes her education. For openers, it's necessary to have as thorough an understanding of sports as possible. If you're working with athletes, you should know what it's like to compete. Playing at any level will help. If you don't play, then try to be as close to sports as you can.

All forms of communication are also very important. That includes writing and public speaking. You'll be communicating through your writing, through one-on-one consultations, and also by speaking to groups. In addition, any psychology courses you can take will be helpful, especially those that will help your counseling skills. And, of course, if you want to be a nutritionist, cooking is another skill you should master.

If you think you might be interested in a career in sports nutrition, you might try to find a sports medicine center where you can do volunteer work or possibly intern with a sports nutritionist. These positions aren't always easy to find. It often depends on where you live and the facilities that are available in your area. Once you complete your schooling, you can look for entry-

Sports nutritionist
Heidi Skolnik
gets her greatest satisfaction from seeing an athlete's performance improve after she's helped change his or her eating patterns. Many athletes have personally thanked her for helping them make this change.

level positions. You may begin by working at a hospital, or perhaps by doing research in an academic setting. There are many things you can do and if you're creative, you can almost make your own niche.

As a sports nutritionist, you work with people who have to be healthy to perform. Your job is to create a nutrition strategy that athletes can use to maximize their training and that allows them to give peak performances for as long as they can. To do this, you have to have a thorough knowledge of nutrition—how foods and groups of foods affect the body and its strength and stamina. You must be able to recommend how athletes should eat when they are on the road, what they must do to lose or gain weight safely, and what they must do to maintain their total well-being.

Your knowledge and research must allow you to differentiate between the specific needs of a particular sport (for example, a baseball player does not have exactly the same nutritional needs as a football or basketball player), and between male and female athletes. You must be able to take your knowledge and your research and apply it.

When you are dealing with an athlete or group of athletes, you have to think, "How can I get my message across?" Many of the people you are counseling have never even thought about nutrition, especially not in the way you are going to explain it. So you have to have a variety of ways to make your point and reinforce it. You can use displays, hand out literature, lecture to entire groups, and provide for one-on-one consultation.

If I am explaining hydration (the absorption of water), for example, I might talk about the necessity for keeping the body properly hydrated during practice and in competition, and the best ways to do it. But I will also explain the qualities of sports drinks that especially help in the hydration process and try to explain, graphically, just what can happen to the body if it is allowed to dehydrate. My goal is that this all-encompassing approach will make the athlete realize the importance of proper hydration in his or her work.

In my work with the New York Giants, I usually spend one day a week with the team and players, both during the season and in the off-season. With the Mets, I work during spring training with the entire organization. I'll spend ten days in Florida with them, then I'm on call during the entire season if a need for my services arises.

What I do for both the Giants and Mets is simply teach the athletes how to eat. I contribute to menu planning, but I'm not involved in every single meal and the foods that are served. Instead, I try to create and encourage nutritional eating patterns. It's not my job to dictate or demand that athletes eat certain foods. The team meals always offer choices. If I'm successful, my counseling will help an athlete to make the best choice.

When I consult with a player on a one-to-one basis, I question his nutritional patterns and try to explain why he may be making the wrong choices. I also tell players that just taking vitamin and mineral supplements is not the answer. Nutrition begins with food and eating patterns, and the supplements are extras.

Being a sports nutritionist presents many challenges and a great deal of hard work. Since I'm often working with clients, I don't go to the office every day. In fact, no two days are alike. I've got to stay up-to-date on all the current research. Since the field is always changing and evolving, I have to know the latest and newest theories and discoveries, and then decide what is best for the athletes.

As a nutritionist, you can't always be with your clients. That's why you've got to have as much knowledge as you can, and be able to present it to an athlete so it's understood completely. That isn't always easy. In addition to everything else, you've got to attend conferences and become involved with organizations that deal with the profession.

It's a never-ending learning process, but it's worth it because you know you are helping people to improve their nutrition and, if they're athletes, to perform better at their jobs.

7 Broadcaster

I began my broadcasting career while I was still attending Southeastern Louisiana University, working at a local radio station and becoming its sports director. Upon graduation, I got my first job, at an NBC affiliate in Hattiesburg, Mississippi, as a part-time week-end sports anchor, earning the grand sum of $5.50 an hour.

Sportscasting began to open up for women in the late 1980s. Phyllis George and Jayne Kennedy were on the *NFL Today* telecasts in the 1970s, but they weren't expected to do "hardcore" reporting. Gayle Gardner, the first woman to become an anchor and reporter at ESPN in the mid-1980s, was perhaps the first woman to really do serious sports reporting. Today networks are simply hiring the best person for the job— sports broadcasting has become an equal-opportunity career.

Now there is a great deal of crossover, with women reporting on men's sports, and men reporting on women's sports. When women were first being hired as broadcast-ers, they were usually relegated to women's sports. But these days, no one really thinks twice about it—as long as the sportscaster is doing a good job.

Gayle Gardner started working for ESPN in the mid-1980s and was one of the first woman broadcasters to do sports reporting on a level with her male colleagues. Here she adds commentary for NBC at Superbowl XXIII in 1989.

I think it's apparent that to be a good sports broadcaster you have to have a real love of sports. When I was a youngster I actually wanted to be a professional athlete. There was always a passion for sports inside of me and I did play sports for many years. But you can love sports with a passion and not be a player.

If you think you may want to go into broadcasting, learn all you can about sports. Read newspapers, sports magazines, and books. You can never know too much. With so much sports coverage on television, you can practice by turning down the sound and calling the games yourself. That's a good early technique, and it's fun. You should also begin learning the basics of writing. Good writing skills are extremely important for any kind of broadcaster, since you'll often be writing your own scripts. Join the school newspaper or yearbook, take English and writing courses, and work hard at them.

Some high schools have their own radio stations, which is a great way to learn. If your school does not, perhaps you can get an internship at a local radio or TV station. When I worked in Mississippi, the station hired kids to go out, get the local sports scores, then come back to the station so they could watch and learn.

A college degree is important for a sports broadcasting career today. This is a very competitive field and the skills you learn at college will be extremely helpful to your career. It isn't always necessary to attend a college with a major communications department or even go to a so-called prestigious university. It's really what you do when you're there that will determine how you fare

afterward. That means doing well in your classes, seeking internships, working at the college or local radio or TV station and getting a well-rounded education.

One thing you should pay attention to is your voice. This has been the biggest knock against women in broadcasting. If you have a high, shrill voice or an accent that reveals the part of the country you're from, you should try to work to improve it. It helps to take speech classes as well as voice and diction lessons, which will help you speak clearly and effectively. While you can't completely change your natural voice, there are subtle changes you can make. You can learn different voice techniques and the correct way to breathe. All this will help, as well as give you the confidence that you have things under control.

If you are determined to forge a career in sports broadcasting, don't be too hasty in turning down jobs in other areas, such as news. Any on-air experience helps. An important thing to remember is to always tape everything you do from your very first job. In broadcasting, your resumé tape is everything. Each time you feel you have a good day, keep a copy of the tape. Your best tapes will help you get an even better job.

It is also important to ask that your work be critiqued by a director in a larger venue. You aren't asking for a job, simply for advice on how to improve. You never know when someone who really likes what he or she hears will happen to have a job opening. You should also try to show versatility in your work. Don't do just news or sports. Do feature stories as well, mixing the themes. Try to include some humorous pieces along with serious ones. That way, you'll show prospective employers your versatility.

Even after you are established in a good position, continue to tape your broadcasts. Then listen to yourself. I always try to maintain a certain level of excellence. It doesn't hurt to pay close attention to others in the field, as well. You can then see and evaluate other approaches and styles.

Sports broadcasting is a challenging profession. You must put in long hours with a great deal of traveling. That can mean being away from family and friends. Of course, the other side of the coin is that the travel can be exciting. You are constantly meeting new people and seeing the world. But broadcasting is a lot more than appearing in front of the camera to give the sports news, or to announce the big game. There

Sitting behind the anchor desk at ESPN means more than just reporting sports news. Hours of preparation take place before I get in front of the camera each time. But when you love sports as much as I do, it often doesn't seem at all like work.

is a great deal of preparation before you go on the air.

Research is very important. Before a game, you've got to research the teams, get to know the players, and try to do some pre-game interviews to pick up little tidbits of information that will make your broadcast more interesting. You also have to make sure you know all the players so that in a fast-paced game, such as basketball, you can identify them in a split second. A broadcaster who doesn't do her homework and isn't well prepared can't fool the listeners for long.

Even if you are working the anchor desk, you must get a solid grasp of the day's stories, do some of your own research, then write your script and learn it before you go on the air. Broadcasting isn't easy. But if you love your work, as I do, and enjoy the competition and

In 1999, Suzyn Waldman became the first woman to do play-by-play in addition to "color" commentary for big-league baseball telecasts. She also is a pioneer in sports radio in New York City. Here she interviews New York Yankees star pitcher David Cone.

personalities, it can be the greatest job in the world.

As a closing piece of advice to any aspiring broadcaster I would simply say this: Don't let anyone tell you that you can't.

This is good advice for anyone in pursuit of a career, including a sports-related career. As you've read, a love of sports and a passion for what you do are two main ingredients to a successful career in sports. Do you have what it takes to be a successful coach, official, journalist, trainer, marketer, nutritionist, or broadcaster? Maybe there are other sports careers to pursue, and perhaps you will invent your own. You already know how much you love sports—let your passion carry you as far as you want to go.

Get in the Game!

There are lots of sites on the World Wide Web that contain information about careers in sports. Use your favorite search engine, and away you go! Here are some good sites to get you started.

www.wnba.com – The official Web site of the WNBA.

www.ncaa.org – The official Web site of the National Collegiate Athletic Association contains many links to other sites, and also lists employment opportunities for the curious.

www.usatrainers.com – The United States Athletic Trainers Organization Web site.

http://pub1.sportsline.com/u/sportscareers/index.html – Part of the CBS Sportsline site, this is a good place to learn about sports careers.

www.nfshsa.org – The National Federation of State High School Athletic Associations site has links to sports medicine, rules, employment, and other areas.

www.coachbasketball.com – Information about and links to the basketball coaching profession.

www.usabasketball.com – Contains information on how to become a certified USA basketball official.

www.eatright.com – The Web site of the American Dietetic Association, which has valuable information on health and nutrition as well as links, including one to careers.

Index